© 2020 Marilu Blau

All Rights Reserved.

ISBN: 978-1-7340281-1-9

All rights reserved. No part of this publication may be reproduced, distributed, or transmitted in any form or by any means, including photocopying, recording, or other electronic or mechanical methods, without the prior written permission of the publisher, except in the case of brief quotations embodied in critical reviews and certain other noncommercial uses permitted by copyright law.
For permission requests, write to the publisher:

BoltonRoadPublishing@gmail.com
Bolton Road Publishing
6395 Pony Express Trail #2
Pollock Pines, CA 95726
530-523-0788

Dedication

In Memory of my parents Mary and Carl Anduri, who gave me such a beautiful childhood, always supported my artistic endeavors and gave me the gift of time to let my imagination run wild.

To my adorable great nieces, Minna, Nicola, and Hazel who gave me inspiration for my stories and paintings.

To Jeff, Danny, Shannon, family, friends, and pets who were always there to encourage me.

Thank you so much to Karen Yeatts and Julie Blau for taking the time to help edit my stories.

Thank you to Darby Patterson. With all her knowledge, experience, and talent, I knew the publishing of my book would be in the perfect hands.

12 Months of Surprises

For Nicola and Minna

By Marilu Blau

January

In January, the New Year begins with Nicola celebrating her birthday! She shares her special day with Minna by ice skating on a little pond in the woods.

As they twirl and glide over the ice, they receive a birthday surprise when their bird friends arrive in the branches above to sing birthday songs.

Their snowman friends gather together and present the birthday girl with a big pink ice cream cake. Nicola shares the cake with Minna and their friends. They celebrate all afternoon.

February

On February 14th, Minna and Nicola put on their Valentine dresses and go for a walk in their favorite park. Before long their squirrel friends appear. They scamper in front of the girls, leading them to a secret garden just for them. When they enter the garden they are surprised to see heart shaped flowers of all sizes and colors.

As the girls admire the flowers, their swan friends glide across the lake towards them bringing baskets full of Valentine treats for everyone to enjoy.

March

The Cherry blossoms are in full bloom, a beautiful sign that March is here. Nicola and Minna are packing their lunch in a picnic basket to share under the cherry trees.

When Nicola and Minna arrive at their favorite spot under the trees, a big surprise is waiting for them. Their cat friends have gotten together and planned a lovely tea party.

Minna serves tea and Nicola serves pink and yellow cupcakes to everyone's delight!

April

It's April, and flowers are blooming, and chicks are hatching. For Easter Sunday, Nicola and Minna are all dressed up in their new Easter dresses. They are so excited for the egg hunt to begin.

This year the Ostriches had decided to give their eggs to the Easter Bunny to color and hide. The Easter Bunny then worked day and night painting the special eggs. He carried them one by one and hid them among the spring flowers.

When the Easter egg hunt begins, Nicola and Minna are so surprised to find the giant colorful eggs. The eggs are so big that only one fits in each basket. They share the rest of the giant eggs with their animal friends. Everyone takes one beautiful egg home, which pleases the Ostriches very much!

May

May is here, and Minna is very excited because her Mommy is expecting a new baby. She waits and waits and finally on May 26th Minna is surprised with a baby sister!

Her name is Hazel and she is very tiny and sweet. Minna can't wait to show Hazel to Nicola. Nicola is so happy to have a new little cousin and Minna is very excited to be a big sister!

June

It is a warm day in June when Nicola and Minna decide to go berry picking. They grab their big shiny buckets. A surprise is waiting for them when they step outside. Their little goat friend is ready to take them to the berry patch in a special wagon.

After an exciting ride down the bumpy path, they finally arrive. There are colorful berries everywhere they look. The girls pick blackberries, raspberries and strawberries until their buckets are overflowing.

Before they head for home, they thank the little goat by feeding him the biggest juiciest strawberry they can find!

July

July is a great month to get away and camp in the mountains. Minna and Nicola are having fun staying in a tent and can't wait until they can have a campfire.

As soon as the sun goes down, the stars and moon appear along with a special surprise. The girls are excited to see their forest friends arrive with sticks and a big bag of marshmallows for toasting over the fire.

They show the girls how to put the marshmallows on the sticks and carefully hold them over the fire until they are golden brown. They all sit around the campfire and eat and eat until it is time to fall asleep under the stars in their cozy little tent.

August

It is August, and Nicola and Minna are happy to be in Hawaii. The first thing they do is run down to the beach. Just as they are heading towards the water they spot their sea turtle friends swimming toward them.

The girls are so excited to see them and especially the surprise they are bringing. The turtles bring the girls a little red boat just their size.

They pull the boat to shore so the girls can have a fun day floating in their boat and playing in the ocean with their friends.

September

September is here, and Minna can't wait to celebrate her birthday with Nicola.

Their Giraffe friend is very pleased with herself because she has made Minna a very special birthday cake. To Minna's surprise, it is the tallest cake she has ever seen. It is so tall that Minna's elephant friend has to lift her up and help her blow out the candles.

Nicola and Hazel help Minna celebrate her special day with balloons and bubbles. Many of their friends join in the celebration and enjoy a big piece of birthday cake!

October

In October, Minna and Nicola pick out costumes to wear for Halloween. Nicola decides to be a black cat and Minna chooses to be a witch.

When Halloween arrives they excitedly put on their costumes and head out to go trick or treating. When they step outside it is so dark they can't see where they are going. Suddenly the sky begins to glow and the girls are so surprised to see their Crow friends bringing orange pumpkin lanterns to light up their way.

They all have a happy and bright Halloween, full of tricks and treats.

November

Fall is here, and the Monarch Butterflies return to their home in the Eucalyptus grove. When they arrive in November, they bring beautiful dresses for Minna and Nicola.

The girls are surprised and delighted to see that their dresses match the colorful wings of their butterfly friends. They put them on and excitedly dance and twirl around and around.

The birds gather in the trees and many of their animal friends come out to watch their performance. It turns out to be a wonderful fall celebration!

December

In December, Minna and Nicola celebrate Santa Lucia Day. In the morning they dress up in white dresses with red sashes. On their heads they wear wreaths made of pine branches with small red candles.

Appearing in their matching dresses, they surprise their Moms and Dads by bringing them freshly baked Swedish buns.

Later that day they receive a surprise of their own when their beautiful and colorful wooden Dala horse friends take them for a ride in the snow to a Christmas tree forest decorated just for them.

They can hardly believe their eyes when they see trees of all colors covered with candles, lights, toys and candy.

Surprises are Great Fun!

What surprises have you had?

And what surprises will

Nicola and Minna have next?

www.ingramcontent.com/pod-product-compliance
Lightning Source LLC
Chambersburg PA
CBHW041819080526

44587CB00004B/141